The Flight of Icarus

by Damian Harvey and Shahab Shamshirsaz

W
FRANKLIN WATTS
LONDON•SYDNEY

The Flight of Icarus

Contents

Chapter 1

The Labyrinth

Daedalus leant against the wall of his cell and sighed.
For many years now, he and his son, Icarus, had been kept
prisoner in this damp, dark tower. Daedalus spent his time
trying to think of how they might get away but so far
he had not been able to come up with a plan, and escape
seemed impossible.

He often thought about the fateful day which had led to his imprisonment. Daedalus had once been an important man: a master craftsman, an inventor and an architect who had built magnificent palaces and temples.

Then one day, King Minos of Crete had commanded Daedalus to appear before him at the royal palace.

Now, Minos was a great and powerful king. His mother, Europa, was a beautiful princess. His father was Zeus, king of all the gods. But even having Zeus as his father hadn't helped King Minos when he had refused to make a sacrifice to honour Poseidon, god of the seas.

Poseidon had been so angry that he'd placed a curse on King Minos and his wife. When their next child was born, it had the head and tail of a bull. Everyone called it the Minotaur, which meant Minos's bull.

As the Minotaur grew bigger and stronger, nobody was able to control him. Day and night, he would charge through the streets of Crete, attacking and killing anyone that got in his way.

Eventually, King Minos decided that something would have to be done about his son. And that was why he had called Daedalus to the palace.

"I want you to build somewhere where my son can be kept safe," said King Minos. "A place where the Minotaur can't hurt anyone and where no one can hurt him."

Daedalus and Icarus knew they needed to build a very special place – a place where no one would ever be able to find the Minotaur. It also had to be a place from which the Minotaur would be unable to escape. They thought and planned, and planned and thought – but at first, none of their ideas seemed to work.

Eventually, they came up with the idea of building a huge labyrinth with hundreds of tunnels, rooms, stairs and doors. They made their plans in secret to make sure no one else would know the layout.

It took Daedalus and his son many years to build the Labyrinth. When they'd finally finished, they proudly showed King Minos their work. They assured him no one who entered the Labyrinth would ever find their way out.

"We are the only ones who have seen the plans," Daedalus told him. "So the secret is safe with us."

King Minos was delighted and had the Minotaur taken to the Labyrinth right away. But instead of rewarding Daedalus and Icarus, he imprisoned them in the high tower. "I am sorry," he told them, "but no one must ever find out the secrets of the Labyrinth, so neither of you will ever be allowed to leave Crete."

Daedalus and Icarus were furious but helpless, and their fate was sealed.

Chapter 2

Prisoners in the Tower

Now, years later, Icarus watched from the top of the tower as a ship headed into the harbour, its huge black sails carrying it along with the wind.

"Look, Father," he called to Daedalus. "A ship from Greece. Perhaps we could escape on a ship like that."

"Perhaps," Daedalus replied. "But first we'd have to get past the guards outside the tower. Then we'd have to reach the ship without being seen."

"Surely we could try," said Icarus. "Anything's better than staying here."

Daedalus shook his head. "Even if we could get away from the guards," he said, "we'd never get to that ship in time.

"Look at its black sails. That ship has come from Athens. It will drop off its passengers, then head back home as quickly as possible."

Sure enough, as they watched, the ship turned around, preparing to head back out to sea. As it sailed away, Daedalus explained that he'd overheard the guards talking about how King Minos had promised not to attack Athens if, every seven years, they sent seven boys and seven girls.

"Are they kept as slaves?" asked Icarus.

"No," Daedalus told him. "They're sent into the Labyrinth as food for the Minotaur."

Icarus looked horrified.

"That's terrible. Someone should do something."

"Well it won't be us," sighed Daedalus. "We have enough problems of our own. I need to think of a way to escape."

"It's useless," said Icarus. "We're trapped here. We'll probably die here too."

But Daedalus was sure there had to be a way. He just needed to discover what that was. Day after day, Daedalus wracked his brains, trying to think of a plan.

Now although they were prisoners, Minos's guards allowed Daedalus and Icarus to wander in the grounds of the tower for exercise. So, while his father was busy thinking, Icarus began to collect things that might be useful. The guards kept a close watch on him so he couldn't go far from their prison, but he still managed to find bits and pieces. Using scraps of material and lengths of thread, Daedalus managed to make a ball of twine.

"It's not strong enough to take our weight," he said, "but perhaps it'll be useful for something else."

"The only way off this island is in a boat," said Icarus, firmly.

"Why do you never listen to me?" said Daedalus.

"You know the guards would stop us before we got anywhere near a boat."

Daedalus reminded his son that King Minos had a huge navy. "We would be lucky to get halfway to Athens before he caught us."

As they talked, an enormous vulture flew past the tower.

They watched in silence as it spread its wings and soared

high into the air.

"That's it!" cried Daedalus. "That's how we'll escape."

Icarus looked puzzled for a moment.

"What do you mean?" he asked.

Daedalus pointed to the vulture,

now far out over the sea.

"We will fly," he said.

"Fly!" cried Icarus, looking

at his father in amazement.

"How can we fly?"

"Like birds of course," Daedalus replied. "We will fly like birds."

Icarus frowned as his father rooted around for pieces of

parchment to write on. "I don't mean to spoil your plan,"

he said, "but we don't have wings."

"Of course we don't," said Daedalus. "We will make them."

Chapter 3

Daedalus's Plan

Icarus watched in silence as Daedalus drew pictures of birds with their wings outstretched.

"I think I have it," said Daedalus. "But we're going to have to work together, and you must listen and do exactly as I say." Icarus listened as Daedalus told him of his plan. "We will build a frame out of wood. The wood will have to be thin but strong," said Daedalus. "Like the bones in a bird's wing."

"Right," said Icarus. "I'll go and see if I can find some wood."

As Icarus turned to go, Daedalus called him back.

"And feathers," he said. "Lots of feathers. As many as you can find."

Icarus was halfway down the tower when he heard his father's voice again.

"Wax!" shouted Daedalus. "We're going to need wax."

As soon as he was outside, Icarus started looking for the things they would need. As he searched, he could see King Minos's guards watching him, suspiciously.

"Hey, Icarus," called one of the guards. "What are you up to? Not trying to escape, are you?"

His companions guffawed at the notion.

"It's cold in the tower at night," Icarus told him. "So I'm collecting wood for a fire."

"And what are you going to do with those?" another guard asked, pointing to the bundle of feathers Icarus had collected.

Icarus thought quickly. "Our beds are too hard and my father's bones are old," he said. "The feathers are for him to lie on."

As the guards nodded, Icarus noticed bits of old candles that had been left on a ledge.

"Can we have those?" he asked. "It's dark in the tower."

"Take them," one of the guards replied. "Though they won't give you much light."

Icarus took the leftover bits of candle and put them in his bag. He even took the dried pieces of wax that had gathered in small puddles at their bases.

Inside the tower, Daedalus made wooden frames with the wood Icarus had found. They reminded Icarus of the skeletons of birds' wings he'd seen washed up on the beach. Despite being big, the frames were light.

"They'll be heavier with the feathers on," said Daedalus. "But with the wind beneath us they'll feel weightless."

"How are we going to attach the feathers?" asked Icarus, holding one up to look at.

Daedalus explained that they would melt the wax and use it like glue, sticking the feathers to the wooden frame. Once the wax dried, it would hold the feathers in place.

Icarus wondered what would happen if the wax got wet, but Daedalus assured him that it didn't matter. "But it will matter if the feathers get wet," he said. "Then we'd be in big trouble."

Daedalus took a feather from Icarus and dipped it into a bowl of water. He handed it back to his son.

Icarus nodded. He could tell right away that the feather was much heavier.

"Remember this," said Daedalus. "When we're in the air, you mustn't get too close to the sea. If your wings get wet you won't be able to fly."

Chapter 4

The Visitor

Icarus and his father worked hard making the wings.
In the mornings, Icarus went to find more feathers.
In the afternoons, he melted the wax while Daedalus
attached them to the frames.

One day, Icarus left some pieces of candle on a window
ledge while he went out. When he got back, the wax had
melted and was dripping on to the floor.

"The sun's hot today," said Icarus. "It's melted these
candles for me."

Daedalus looked up at the sun and nodded, thoughtfully.

"So, we've learnt another important lesson," he said.

"A lesson you need to remember."

"Don't leave candles on the window ledge?" said Icarus.

"No," his father replied. "When we're in the air, we

mustn't fly too close to the sun or our wings will melt."

Just then, they heard a voice calling them from the bottom of the tower. The voice was followed by the sound of footsteps.

"Quick!" whispered Daedalus. "We can't let anyone see what we're doing."

Closing the door behind them, Icarus and Daedalus made their way down the stairs to meet their visitor. Daedalus was surprised to see that it was Princess Ariadne, one of King Minos's daughters.

"Princess, has your father sent you?" Daedalus asked.

"No!" the princess replied. "My father would be angry if he knew I was here. I've come to ask for your help."

The princess told them that she had fallen in love with an Athenian prince called Theseus.

"Your father won't like that," said Daedalus.

"That isn't the problem," Ariadne replied.

"Then what is it?" asked Icarus.

Ariadne told them that Theseus had arrived in Crete on board a ship from Athens. Even though he had been in disguise, Ariadne had recognised him straight away. She had seen him before when visiting Athens with her father.

"Now I understand," said Daedalus. "Theseus is going to be thrown into the Labyrinth for the Minotaur."

"What's this got to do with us?" asked Icarus.

"Theseus is planning to kill the Minotaur then escape to Athens," said Ariadne. "And he's taking me with him."

Knowing that this was impossible, Daedalus laughed. "He'll never find his way out of the Labyrinth," he said.

"That's why I need your help," Ariadne told him.

Icarus shook his head. "Only my father and I know the secrets of the Labyrinth, and we promised King Minos that we'd never tell a soul about it," he said. "The king will know we've helped you and he'll surely have us put to death."

"But there must be a way," said Ariadne. "Theseus will die without your help."

Daedalus couldn't help feeling sorry for the princess. "Perhaps there is a way we can help without breaking our promise," he said.

Daedalus gave Ariadne the ball of twine they'd made. "Give this to Theseus before he goes into the Labyrinth tonight," he said. "He should tie one end near the door, then let it unravel as he goes in. When he wants to get out, he can follow the twine back."

As they watched the princess leave, Daedalus couldn't help feeling that he might have made a big mistake.

"Oh well," he sighed. "Come on. We must get on with the wings."

Chapter 5

Flying High

Icarus and his father worked late into the night to make sure the wings were finished. The next morning, Icarus was awakened by his father.

"Quick!" said Daedalus. "King Minos is coming with his soldiers. We have to go!" Icarus and Daedalus carried their wings out on to the top of the tower. Sure enough, Icarus could see King Minos and his men heading towards them.

Daedalus helped Icarus put on his wings, fastening
the leather straps to hold them in place. "When I woke,
I saw a ship leaving the harbour," Daedalus told him. "I had
a feeling it might be Theseus escaping with Princess Ariadne.
Then, when I saw King Minos coming this way, I knew
for certain."

"You mean Theseus has killed the Minotaur?" said Icarus.

"Yes!" Daedalus replied, putting on his own wings.

"And now King Minos is coming to kill us."

Behind them, they could already hear the sound of
footsteps climbing the tower. There wasn't a moment to
lose. Together, Icarus and Daedalus leaped from the top
of the tower.

The wind lifted Daedalus high into the air, but Icarus
let out a loud cry as he fell. The wind was rushing through
his hair and the rocks below were getting closer.
Any second now he would crash on to them.

"Open your wings," shouted Daedalus.

Icarus heard his father and spread his arms as wide as he could. As he did, the wind took hold of him and lifted him high into the air. "I'm flying!" he shouted. "I'm flying!"

Behind them they could see King Minos and his guards at the top of the tower. They'd only jumped from it a moment ago but they were already out of reach.

"We're free!" shouted Icarus. "We're free!"

"Not yet we're not," said Daedalus. "We've still got a long way to go."

Far below, Icarus spotted a small fishing boat bobbing about on the water. He could see the fishermen gazing up at them. "We must look like winged gods to them," he said.

Icarus folded back his wings and swooped down towards the boat.

"Don't go too close to the water," Daedalus shouted.

Icarus whizzed over the fishing boat then soared back up into the air.

"Don't worry," he told Daedalus. "Flying is easy ... I know what I'm doing."

Flapping his huge wings, Icarus went up past his father.

"Remember what I said, Icarus. Don't go too high," Daedalus reminded him. "If you get too close to the sun, the wax will melt."

But Icarus wasn't listening. Higher and higher he went, flapping his huge wings.

"Look at me," he called, but Daedalus couldn't hear him. Icarus had gone too high.

Suddenly, Icarus spotted a feather falling down from his wings. Then another, and another.

"No!" Icarus cried. But it was too late. The heat of the sun was melting the wax and his wings were falling apart.

Icarus stopped climbing and started to fall. He flapped his wings but it was no use. With each flap, clumps of feathers fell away.

Soon Icarus was plummeting down. Faster and faster

he went until ... SPLASH!

He hit the water far below.

Daedalus saw his son falling from the sky and flew down

as quickly as he could. He searched back and forth over

the waves but there was no sign of Icarus anywhere.

There was nothing left now for Daedalus to do.

With a heavy heart, he spread his wings and flew onward.

If only his son had listened to him ...

Things to think about

1. How do you think Daedalus and Icarus felt about being imprisoned in the tower after building the Labyrinth?
2. What impression do you have of King Minos after reading this story?
3. Do you think that Icarus does listen to his father in the story? Do they work well as a team?
4. Why do you think the guards allow Icarus to collect all the things they need to build the wings?
5. Why do you think Icarus flies too close to the sun at the end of the story?

Write it yourself

This book retells the famous Greek myth of Icarus and Daedalus, and their escape from the tower. Now try to write your own retelling of a different myth you know.

Plan your story before you begin to write it.

Start off with a story map:

- a beginning to introduce the characters and where and when your story is set (the setting);
- a problem which the main characters will need to fix in the story;
- an ending where the problems are resolved.

Get writing! Try to include geographical and historical details so that your readers get a sense of the time and place of your story, and think about the dialogue your characters would use. Would they use formal or informal language?

Notes for parents and carers

Independent reading
The aim of independent reading is to read this book with ease. This series is designed to provide an opportunity for your child to read for pleasure and enjoyment. These notes are written for you to help your child make the most of this book.

About the book
This retelling of the famous Greek myth brings to life the story of Icarus and Daedalus, their imprisonment in the tower by King Minos and their daring plan to escape.

Before reading
Ask your child why they have selected this book. Look at the title and blurb together. What do they think it will be about? Do they think they will like it?

During reading
Encourage your child to read independently. If they get stuck on a longer word, remind them that they can find syllable chunks that can be sounded out from left to right. They can also read on in the sentence and think about what would make sense.

After reading
Support comprehension by talking about the story. What happened?
Then help your child think about the messages in the book that go beyond the story, using the questions on the page opposite. Give your child a chance to respond to the story, asking:
Did you enjoy the story and why? Who was your favourite character?
What was your favourite part? What did you expect to happen at the end?

Franklin Watts
First published in Great Britain in 2019
by The Watts Publishing Group

Series Editors: Jackie Hamley and Melanie Palmer
Series Advisors: Dr Sue Bodman and Glen Franklin
Series Designer: Peter Scoulding

A CIP catalogue record for this book is
available from the British Library.

ISBN 978 1 4451 6531 8 (hbk)
ISBN 978 1 4451 6532 5 (pbk)
ISBN 978 1 4451 7033 6 (library ebook)

Printed in China

Franklin Watts
An imprint of
Hachette Children's Group
Part of The Watts Publishing Group
Carmelite House
50 Victoria Embankment
London EC4Y 0DZ

An Hachette UK Company
www.hachette.co.uk

www.franklinwatts.co.uk